Cordon Bleu
Appetisers

Cordon Bleu Minibooks/Macdonald Unit 75

These recipes have been adapted from the *Cordon Bleu Cookery Course* published by Purnell in association with the London Cordon Bleu Cookery School.

Principal: Rosemary Hume; Co-Principal: Muriel Downes

Cover photo: Terrine maison (see pages 44–45)

© 1971 BPC Publishing Ltd.
Published by Macdonald Unit 75
49 Poland Street, London W1A 2LG

Made and printed in Great Britain
by Taylowe Ltd., Maidenhead

Designed by Melvyn Kyte

SBN 356 03485 2

Contents

Glossary

Au bain marie	To cook at a temperature just below boiling point in a bain marie (a tin or pan standing in a larger pan of simmering water); may be carried out in oven or on top of stove.
Clarified butter	Heat butter gently until foaming, strain well, then pour off the clear yellow oil, leaving sediment (milk solids) in pan; skim oil well and leave to solidify before use.
Farce	Stuffing, of various kinds.
Fritter batter	Sift 6 tablespoons flour with a pinch of salt, make a well in the centre and add 3 egg yolks, $1\frac{1}{2}$ tablespoons melted butter, or oil, and mix with $7\frac{1}{2}$ fl oz milk to a smooth batter; beat thoroughly. Stand in a cool place for 30 minutes. Just before frying, whisk 2 egg whites stiffly and fold into batter.
Frying temperatures	Minimum temperature for frying is 340°F. Oil must never be heated above 375°F, and for sunflower oil and some commercially prepared fats (e.g. Spry, Cookeen) 360°F is the highest recommended temperature.
Refresh	To pour cold water over previously blanched and drained food. This sets vegetable colours and cleans meat/offal.
Tartare sauce	Make by rubbing 2 hard-boiled egg yolks through a strainer and adding one raw egg yolk; then add $\frac{1}{2}$ pint of oil, drop by drop. Dilute sauce, if necessary, with a little vinegar and flavour with chopped capers or gherkins, parsley and chives.

General rule: all recipes are tested at the *Cordon Bleu Cookery School* in London and quantities are sufficient for 4 servings. Spoon measures are level unless otherwise stated.

Grilled grapefruit

2 grapefruit
4 tablespoons sherry
4 dessertspoons soft, light
  brown sugar
1 oz butter ($\frac{1}{4}$ oz per person)

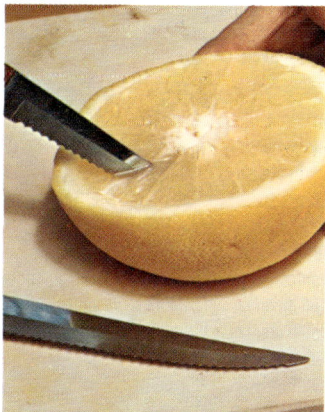

Method

Prepare the halved grapefruit in the following way. Using a small sharp knife, preferably with a curved and serrated blade, first cut out the core, then run the knife round the outside edge of the grapefruit, cutting between the flesh and the pith. Then slip knife either side of each membrane and lift out carefully without disturbing the segments of grapefruit; with practice this is done very speedily and easily. Carefully remove any pips.

Sprinkle each half with the sherry and set in a dish ready for grilling. This can be done several hours before the meal.

Pre-heat grill, sprinkle sugar over the grapefruit halves and dot with butter; cook until the sugar is lightly caramelised (browned but not burnt). Serve hot.

Before grilling grapefruit, remove the core and cut the flesh away from the pith. Slip the knife very carefully down sides of the membranes to separate each of the segments

Artichokes vinaigrette

4 globe artichokes

For vinaigrette dressing
2 shallots (finely chopped)
6 tablespoons olive oil
2–3 oz mushrooms (finely
  chopped)
3 tablespoons white wine
2 tablespoons white wine
  vinegar
salt and pepper
squeeze of lemon juice
  (optional)
1 clove of garlic (optional)
3 oz ham (thinly sliced and
  finely chopped)
1 tablespoon chopped parsley,
  or chopped mixed herbs

Method

Trim off the points and leaves of the artichokes with scissors and trim the stalk from the bottom. Plunge artichokes into boiling salted water and boil gently until a leaf can be pulled out (about 35–40 minutes). Then drain, and refresh.

Meanwhile prepare the dressing. Sauté the shallots slowly until just tender in 2 tablespoons of the oil, add the mushrooms and cook for 2–3 minutes. Turn into a bowl and leave until cool, then add wine, vinegar and remaining oil. Season well and add a squeeze of lemon juice if the dressing is not sharp enough. Flavour with a little garlic, if liked, and add the ham. Leave this to marinate for 15–20 minutes.

Prepare each artichoke by pulling out some of the centre leaves until the choke can be reached; carefully scrape this away with a dessertspoon. Put a spoonful of the dressing in the centre of each artichoke, set them on individual dishes and dust with the chopped parsley or herbs. Serve cold.

Chopped shallots, mushrooms and ham are mixed with wine, vinegar and oil to make a thick dressing for the artichokes

After some of the centre leaves and the chokes have been removed, the vinaigrette dressing is spooned into the artichokes

Asparagus nordaise

1 bundle of asparagus
2 oz mushrooms
$1\frac{1}{4}$ oz butter
salt and pepper
$\frac{1}{2}$ oz flour
5 fl oz top of milk
$1\frac{1}{2}$ oz grated cheese
hot buttered toast (for serving)

This quantity makes approximately 8 servings.

Method

Trim the asparagus stalks to within 2–3 inches of the green, and tie into a bundle. Boil in plenty of salted water for 12–15 minutes, or until tender. The heads of the asparagus should be upwards, and if the tips are out of water, cook with the pan lid on. If the tips are underwater, cook with the pan lid off. Drain well. Wash and cut the mushrooms into thick slices, add to $\frac{3}{4}$ oz of the butter, melted; season and cook slowly with the pan lid on for 5–6 minutes.

Melt the remaining $\frac{1}{2}$ oz butter in a pan, add the flour, mix together, then pour on the milk. Stir sauce until boiling; add the cheese and seasoning.

Arrange the mushrooms, and then 1–2 asparagus tips, on fingers of hot buttered toast. Spoon sauce over each one and glaze them under the grill.

Stuffed avocado pears

3 avocado pears
1 packet of cream cheese
   (2–3 oz)
1–2 teaspoons anchovy essence
6 black olives (chopped)
juice of 1 lemon
lettuce leaves (to garnish)
$\frac{1}{4}$ pint vinaigrette dressing
   (see page 6)

Method

Work the cream cheese with the anchovy essence and add the chopped olives. Halve, skin and remove the stones from the avocados. Fill the cavities with the cream cheese mixture and re-shape. Roll each avocado quickly in the lemon juice and wrap in transparent wrapping paper (Saran wrap) or wet greaseproof paper to exclude the air. Keep them refrigerated until ready to serve.

Arrange crisp lettuce leaves on a serving platter, slice the avocados in rounds, place on the lettuce and spoon over the vinaigrette dressing.

Aubergine with crab

2 good-size aubergines
6–7 oz crab claw meat
salt and pepper
oil
2 medium-size onions
1 dessertspoon paprika pepper
1 tablespoon tomato purée
$\frac{1}{2}$ lb ripe tomatoes (skinned,
    seeds removed, and sliced)
$\frac{1}{2}$ teaspoon oregano
pinch of cayenne pepper,
    or drop of Tabasco sauce
2 tablespoons grated Parmesan
    and Gruyère cheese (mixed)
1–2 tablespoons melted butter

Method

Split aubergines in two lengthways, score, sprinkle with salt and leave for 30 minutes. Set oven at 350°F or Mark 4.

Wipe aubergines dry, then brown the cut surface in a little hot oil; take out, set on a baking tin and cook in pre-set moderate oven until tender (about 10 minutes).

Meanwhile slice onions and soften in 2–3 tablespoons oil; add paprika and after a few seconds add tomato purée, tomatoes, oregano and cayenne (or Tabasco). Season and cook to a rich pulp. Scoop out the pulp from the cooked aubergines, add it to the pan and continue to cook for a few minutes. Then flake the crab meat with a fork and add it to the pan. Pile this mixture into the aubergine skins, sprinkle well with cheese and melted butter and bake in quick oven (425°F or Mark 7) for 6–7 minutes to brown.

Aubergine with crab: aubergines stuffed with onion, tomato and flaked crab meat

Eggs Jacqueline

4 eggs
1½ oz butter
½ teaspoon paprika pepper
6 oz shelled prawns
salt and pepper
1 packet (about 12 oz)
    frozen asparagus
½ pint béchamel sauce
    (see page 19)

To finish

1 tablespoon grated
    Parmesan cheese

Method

Hard boil the eggs and cut them in two lengthways. Sieve the yolks and place the whites in a bowl of cold water. Cream the butter with the paprika and mix with the yolks, adding 2 oz of the prawns, finely chopped. Season to taste. Cook the asparagus following the instructions on the packet, drain, refresh it with cold water to set the colour and drain again.

Prepare the béchamel sauce, season to taste and simmer for 2—3 minutes. Place the asparagus in a buttered ovenproof dish, fill the egg whites with the prawn mixture and place on the asparagus. Scatter the remaining prawns (whole) on top. Coat the filled eggs with the béchamel sauce, sprinkle with the cheese and bake in hot oven at 400°F or Mark 6 for 15—20 minutes until golden-brown.

The finished dish, with some of the ingredients for eggs Jacqueline

Salad Clémentine

6 tomatoes
salt and pepper
2 tablespoons salad oil
6 eggs (hard-boiled and sliced)
1 tablespoon capers
1 tablespoon gherkins (sliced)
6 anchovy fillets
brown bread and butter
   (for serving)

For dressing

2 tablespoons wine vinegar
1 teaspoon dry mustard
6 tablespoons salad oil
3 dessertspoons tomato
   ketchup
1 tablespoon mixed herbs
   (fresh parsley, chives and
   mint, or 1 tablespoon parsley
   and pinch of dried mixed
   herbs) – chopped
salt
black pepper (ground from
   mill)

Method

Scald and skin the tomatoes, cut in half through the stalk, cut out the small piece of core at the stalk end and remove seeds. Season tomatoes lightly. Heat oil in a pan and sauté tomatoes very quickly on each side; lift out very carefully and leave to cool.

Peel and slice the eggs and arrange them in the bottom of an entrée dish, scatter the capers and gherkins over them. Set the tomatoes, cut side downwards, on top.

Split the anchovies in half and soak them in 2 tablespoons milk to remove excess salt.

Combine the ingredients for the dressing, adding salt and black pepper to taste.

Drain the anchovy fillets and arrange them lattice-wise over the tomatoes; pour over the dressing. Chill salad in refrigerator for 1 hour before serving with slices of brown bread and butter.

Watchpoint Tomatoes, even if very ripe, must be sautéd in the oil for this dish. If this is not done they make too much juice when standing after the dressing is poured on.

Decorating the tomatoes with anchovy fillets, before adding dressing

Melon salad

1 honeydew melon
1 lb tomatoes
1 large cucumber
salt
1 tablespoon parsley
   (chopped)
1 heaped teaspoon mint
   and chives (chopped)

For French dressing

2 tablespoons wine vinegar
salt and pepper
caster sugar
6 tablespoons salad oil

Method

Cut the melon in half, remove the seeds and scoop out the flesh with a vegetable cutter or cut into cubes.

Skin and quarter the tomatoes, squeeze out the seeds and remove the core; cut quarters again if the tomatoes are large.

Peel the cucumber, cut in small cubes, or the same size as the melon cubes. Sprinkle lightly with salt, cover with a plate and stand for 30 minutes; drain away any liquid and rinse cubes with cold water.

To prepare the dressing: mix the vinegar, seasoning and sugar together, whisk in oil.

Mix the fruit and vegetables together in a deep bowl (or soup tureen), pour over the dressing, cover and chill for 2–3 hours.

Just before serving, mix in the herbs. Serve from the bowl or tureen with a ladle, into soup cups.

While standing, the salad will make a lot of juice, so it should be eaten with a spoon. You'll find a hot herb loaf goes well with melon salad.

Hot herb loaf

1 French loaf
4 oz butter
1 tablespoon mixed dried herbs
juice of $\frac{1}{4}$ lemon
black pepper
little garlic (crushed) – optional

Method

Cream the butter with the herbs, lemon juice and seasoning; if you like garlic, add a little now.

Cut the loaf in even, slanting slices about $\frac{1}{2}$-inch thick; spread each slice generously with the butter mixture and reshape the loaf, spreading any remaining butter over the top and sides before wrapping in foil.

Bake for 10 minutes in a hot oven at 425°F or Mark 7. Then reduce oven setting to 400°F or Mark 6, and open the foil so that the bread browns and crisps. This should take a further 5–8 minutes.

2 large smooth-skinned grapefruit
about 3–4 stems of ginger in syrup (sliced, or shredded)

Method

Halve the grapefruit and prepare in the usual way, removing all the pith (see page 5). Hollow the centre slightly and then put 1 tablespoon of sliced ginger with a teaspoon of the syrup in the centre of each half. Chill and serve in coupe glasses.

Artichokes à la crème Béchamel sauce

1 can (14 oz) artichoke hearts
¾ pint béchamel sauce
Parmesan cheese (grated) – for
   dusting

Buttered ramekins, or individual dishes

Method
Set oven at 400°F or Mark 6.
Drain artichoke hearts, arrange
in buttered dishes. Make
béchamel sauce, pour over
artichokes and dust with grated
Parmesan. Bake in pre-set oven
for 10–12 minutes, or until
lightly browned.

Infuse ¾ pint of milk with a
slice of onion, 6 peppercorns,
1 blade of mace and 1 bayleaf
over a low heat for 5–7 minutes, but do not boil. Pour
milk into a basin and wipe the
pan out.

Melt 1 oz butter slowly,
remove pan from heat and stir
in 2 tablespoons flour. Pour on
at least one-third of the milk
through a strainer and blend
in with a wooden spoon. Add
the rest of the milk, season
lightly, return to heat and stir
until boiling. Boil for not more
than 2 minutes, then adjust
seasoning. This sauce may be
finished with 1 tablespoon of
cream.

Pineapple jelly salad

1 large can (approximately
    24 fl oz) pineapple juice
juice of 2 large oranges
    (strained)
2 wineglasses dry white wine,
    or water
1 tablespoon white wine
    vinegar
1 oz gelatine (soaked in 5–6
    tablespoons cold water)
    – see note on page 22
6 tablespoons canned
    pineapple (diced)
1 bunch of watercress

For dressing
2 packets of Demi-Sel
    cheese, or 4 oz cream
    cheese
¼ pint single cream
salt and pepper

Ring mould (2–2½ pints capacity)

Method
Combine the pineapple and strained orange juices with the wine (or water) and vinegar in a large pan.

Watchpoint Do not use the syrup from a can of pineapple pieces because this would be too sweet.

Make up this liquid to 1½ pints with more juice or water, if necessary.

Dissolve the soaked gelatine in a pan and when quite hot add to the liquid; pour about one-third into the wet mould and leave in a cold place until almost set.

Arrange diced pineapple in the mould and fill up with remaining cool, but still liquid, jelly. Cover and leave for 2–3 hours in refrigerator or overnight in a cool larder before turning out.

To prepare dressing: rub cheese through a wire strainer into a bowl and beat in the cream a little at a time. Season to taste, then pour the dressing into a small bowl or sauce boat for serving.

Turn out the jelly on to a flat serving

plate and fill the centre with watercress.
Watchpoint To turn out the jelly, dip the mould quickly in and out of a bowl containing hot water. Wipe the outside of the mould and then put the plate over the top and turn it upside down. Holding the plate and mould, give them a smart shake from side to side (not up and down, which would spoil the shape), then lift away the mould.

Serve with brown bread and butter and the dressing separately.

Below, left: arranging diced pineapple over gelatine mixture in mould
Below: dipping mould in hot water to loosen jelly

Note: Gelatine is made from the bones and tissues of animals or fish by prolonged boiling. It is used to set jellies and cream sweets. It is sold in powdered form and as thick leaf and fine French leaf. Powdered gelatine is soaked in the liquid specified in the recipe, and then dissolved in the same liquid.

Thick leaf and French leaf are soaked in water until soft, drained and then dissolved in the liquid specified in recipe before use.

As few spoons are standard in size it is safer to measure gelatine in ounces, but as a rough guide 2 level (not rounded) tablespoons powdered gelatine equal 1 oz; 2 sheets of strip (thick leaf), or 6 sheets of French leaf, gelatine equal 1 oz.

Quantities required to set 2 pints of liquid.

$\frac{3}{4}$–2 oz powdered gelatine
$1\frac{3}{4}$–2 oz French leaf gelatine
$1\frac{1}{2}$ oz strip (thick leaf) gelatine
$\frac{1}{2}$ oz agar-agar
1 oz isinglass

Mushrooms au gratin

1 lb mushrooms
1–1½ oz butter
salt and pepper
pinch of mace
cayenne pepper

For sauce

1 oz butter
1 oz flour
7½ fl oz milk
2½ fl oz double cream
2–3 tablespoons browned crumbs
2–3 tablespoons grated Parmesan
  cheese

Method

Trim, wash and dry the mushrooms (leaving on the stalks), and fry briskly in the butter. Turn into a gratin dish, season with salt, pepper, mace and a sprinkling of cayenne pepper.

For sauce, melt butter, add the flour, mix together, then pour on the milk. Stir until boiling. Add cream after the sauce has boiled for 1 minute.

Spoon sauce over the mushrooms, dust with crumbs and Parmesan cheese. Bake in pre-set oven, at 400°F or Mark 6, for 7–10 minutes.

Scallop chowder

4 large scallops
4 oz long grain rice
about 1 oz butter
1 medium-size onion
   (finely chopped)
4 oz streaky bacon rashers
   (rind and rust removed –
   cut into strips)
1 small head of celery
   (finely sliced)
1 small can (8 oz) tomatoes
about 1½ pints boiling water
large pinch of saffron (infused
   in 2 tablespoons hot water
   for about 30 minutes)
salt
pepper (ground from mill)
1 tablespoon chopped parsley

Method

Soak the rice in a little cold water for about 30 minutes and then drain. Melt the butter in a large saucepan, put in the onion and bacon and fry gently for a few minutes, then add the rice and continue to fry gently for 1–2 minutes more. Add the celery, tomatoes, boiling water and saffron. Season, partially cover the pan and simmer until the rice is very tender, about 15–20 minutes.

Slice the scallops crosswise and add them to the soup. Taste for seasoning and continue to simmer for a further 15–20 minutes. Just before serving stir in the parsley.

Note: if wished, a glass of white wine may be added in place of an equal quantity of the boiling water. The chowder should be fairly thick but not too much so; more liquid should be added if too much reduction takes place.

Whitings Orly

3–4 whitings
   (about 12 oz filleted)
squeeze of lemon juice
seasoned flour
$\frac{1}{2}$–$\frac{3}{4}$ pint fritter batter
   (see Glossary)
deep fat (for frying)

Method

Skin the fillets, lay them on a plate and sprinkle lightly with a little lemon juice. Leave in the refrigerator for about 1 hour. Then dab the fillets with absorbent paper to dry and cut each one into diagonal strips about 1 inch or more in width.

To fry the whitings, first roll them in seasoned flour. Have the batter ready. Heat the fat bath until at frying temperature (see Glossary). Put a few pieces of the fish into the batter. Turn round lightly with a flat whisk or fork, lift out and drop carefully into the fat. Fry about 6–8 pieces at a time; when golden-brown, lift out and drain on absorbent paper, or a cooling rack set over a baking sheet, then set aside. Continue until all the pieces of fish are fried, dish up and serve either a sweet pimiento sauce, or a tartare sauce (see Glossary), separately.

Sweet pimiento sauce

2 egg yolks
1 hard-boiled egg yolk (sieved)
$\frac{1}{2}$ teaspoon paprika pepper
salt and pepper
dash of Tabasco sauce
grated rind of $\frac{1}{2}$ orange
$7\frac{1}{2}$ fl oz olive, or salad, oil
about 1 dessertspoon vinegar (to taste)
2 small caps of canned pimiento (or 1 large one)
  – finely chopped, or rubbed through a sieve
1 tablespoon juice from pimiento can
1 tablespoon double cream (optional)

Method
Put the egg yolks, both raw and hard-boiled, into a bowl. Work with the seasonings and orange rind, then gradually add the oil as if making mayonnaise. When it begins to get too thick, add the vinegar. When all the oil is mixed in, add the chopped strained pimientos. Finish with the juice and the cream, if used, and adjust seasoning.

*Whitings Orly with
sweet pimiento sauce*

Mushrooms in white wine

1 lb mushrooms
2 oz butter, or 3 tablespoons
  olive oil
2 large onions (finely sliced)
2 wineglasses white wine
bouquet garni
salt
pepper (ground from mill)
1 tablespoon chopped
  parsley

To serve

crisp rolls and unsalted
  butter

Method

Trim the mushrooms, wash quickly in salted water and cut in thick slices. Heat the butter (or oil) in a sauté pan, add the mushrooms, sauté over a quick heat for 1–2 minutes then remove from the pan. Reduce the heat, add the onions to pan and cook slowly until soft but not coloured; tip on the white wine, add the bouquet garni and simmer until the wine is reduced by half. Return the mushrooms to the pan, season with salt and pepper from the mill and simmer for 5 minutes. Remove bouquet garni, tip the mushroom mixture into a hot gratin dish and dust with parsley.

Serve with hot rolls and butter.

Slicing the onions and mushrooms after trimming and washing

Adding sauté mushrooms to pan with onions, wine and herbs

Prawn pilaf

8 oz long grain rice
pinch of saffron
1 onion (finely sliced)
2 oz butter
salt and pepper
$1\frac{1}{4}$–$1\frac{1}{2}$ pints chicken stock,
 or bouillon cubes
2 tablespoons Parmesan
 cheese (grated)

For prawn salpicon

8 oz prawns (shelled)
1 oz butter
1 shallot (finely chopped)
8 oz tomatoes
1 teaspoon paprika
1 teaspoon tomato purée
salt
pepper (ground from mill)
pinch of sugar
few whole prawns (optional)

*7-inch diameter border, or ring,
mould ($1\frac{1}{4}$-pints capacity)*

Method

Set the oven at 375°F or Mark 5 and butter the border, or ring, mould. Soak saffron in an egg cup of boiling water for 30 minutes.

Slice the onion finely, put into a pan with two-thirds of the butter, cover and cook slowly until soft but not coloured. Add the rice and fry for 2–3 minutes until it looks almost transparent. Then add the saffron and its liquid, seasoning and $1\frac{1}{4}$ pints of stock. Bring to the boil, stir once with a fork, then cover; put in the oven and cook for 20–30 minutes or until rice is tender and the stock absorbed. Look at the rice after 20 minutes and if it is not quite tender but all the stock has been absorbed, add the extra $\frac{1}{4}$ pint of chicken stock.

When rice is cooked remove from oven, dot the remaining butter over the top, dust with the cheese, cover and leave to absorb these for 5–10 minutes.

Meanwhile prepare the salpicon. Melt the butter in a pan, add chopped shallot, cover and cook slowly until soft. Scald, skin and quarter the tomatoes and scoop out the seeds; rub seeds in a strainer and keep the juice. Add paprika to the shallot, cook for 1 minute, then stir in the tomato purée and juice from the seeds. Season and add a pinch of sugar. Simmer for 2—3 minutes. Add shelled prawns and tomatoes to the pan and toss well over the heat.

Stir the topping of butter and cheese into the rice with a fork and then spoon pilaf carefully into the buttered border, or ring, mould; press lightly, turn on to a hot serving dish and spoon the prawn salpicon into the centre of the pilaf. Garnish with whole prawns if wished.

After turning rice out of the ring mould, carefully spoon the prawn salpicon mixture into the centre. You can then add whole prawns — not shelled — for decoration

Shrimps Mariette

4 oz shelled fresh, or frozen,
  shrimps
round croûtes of bread (1–1½
  inches in diameter
salt
pinch of pepper, or cayenne
  pepper, or Tabasco sauce
½ oz butter

For cheese cream

½ oz butter
½ oz flour
¼ pint creamy milk
1½ oz cheese (grated)
salt and pepper
English mustard

Method
Heat some oil or butter and fry
the croûtes until golden-
brown, drain and keep warm.
Toss the shrimps over the heat
with the seasoning and butter
and, when this mixture is
thoroughly hot, pile it up on
the croûtes. Put these in a
flameproof dish and keep warm
while preparing the cheese
cream. Proceed as if making a
white sauce (see page 23);
finish by gradually beating in
the grated cheese. Season
lightly and add mustard to
taste. Spoon this cheese cream
over the prepared croûtes and
brown well under the grill.
Serve very hot.

*Shrimps Mariette make an un-
usual appetiser, served hot*

Roulades of smoked salmon

1 small brown loaf
about 4 oz butter
½ lb smoked salmon
juice of ½ lemon
black pepper (ground from mill)

Method
Cut the crust lengthways from the top of the loaf; butter and cut thin slices from the length of the loaf. Cover each slice with smoked salmon and season with lemon juice and pepper. Trim away crust and roll each slice the length of the loaf like a swiss roll. Then cut each roll in thin slices.

Watchpoint If the bread is crumbly, it will be easier to slice the rolls if they are first wrapped in greaseproof paper and chilled.

Slice roulades of smoked salmon thinly before serving

Curried fish croquettes

½ lb fresh haddock fillet
1 blade of mace
1 oz butter
1 shallot (finely chopped)
1 teaspoon curry powder
1 oz flour
4 fl oz milk
salt and pepper
½ egg (beaten)
deep fat (for frying)

For coating

1 egg (beaten)
dried white breadcrumbs

Method

Poach the haddock, with the mace to flavour, in moderate oven at 350°F or Mark 4 for 10–15 minutes or until tender, then drain, remove skin and bones, and flake flesh. Melt half the butter, add the shallot and cook for 2–3 minutes. Add the curry powder and cook a further minute. Blend in the flour and milk, stir over heat until boiling and allow to simmer for a minute or so. Put flaked fish into the sauce a little at a time. Season to taste and add beaten egg. Turn mixture on to a plate and allow it to get quite cold. Divide it into dessertspoonfuls and roll into croquettes (cork shapes) on a floured board. Coat with egg and crumbs; fry in deep fat until crisp and golden-brown.

Sole bonne femme

4 double, or 8 single, fillets
 of Dover, or lemon, sole
6 peppercorns
1 slice of onion
1 bayleaf
1 wineglass white wine
1 wineglass water
2 oz mushrooms (trimmed,
 washed and sliced)
squeeze of lemon juice

For hollandaise sauce

1 onion (sliced)
2 tablespoons tarragon
 vinegar
1 egg yolk (beaten)
2 oz butter

For white wine sauce

1 oz butter
1 rounded tablespoon flour
$7\frac{1}{2}$ fl oz fish stock (using
 white wine, see method)
5 tablespoons top of the milk
salt and pepper

Method

First prepare the hollandaise sauce: add sliced onion to vinegar and reduce to 1 teaspoon over gentle heat. Strain on to the beaten yolk, standing bowl in a bain marie; add $\frac{1}{4}$ oz butter and beat until thick. Then

add the rest of the butter slowly, beating well. When the consistency is of thick cream, cover and set aside.

Set oven at 350°F or Mark 4.

To prepare the sole: skin, wash and dry the fillets, fold in half lengthways, put in a buttered ovenproof dish, add peppercorns, onion slice and bayleaf, pour over the white wine and water. Cover with buttered paper and poach in pre-set oven for 15–20 minutes. Strain the liquid from the fish and measure it – there should be about $7\frac{1}{2}$ fl oz of stock.

To make white wine sauce: melt the butter in a saucepan, add the flour – off the heat – then pour on the fish stock. Stir until thick, add milk and bring quickly to the boil.

Left: straining vinegar on to beaten egg yolk for the hollandaise sauce
Right: the finished hollandaise sauce should have the consistency of thick cream

Adjust seasoning and simmer sauce for 2—3 minutes to a coating consistency.

Cook mushrooms quickly in 1 table-spoon of water and a squeeze of lemon juice. Put fillets on serving dish, coat with the white wine sauce, scatter on the mushrooms and then put a tablespoon of the hollandaise on each fillet. Glaze under the grill and serve sole at once.

Above right: pouring wine over fillets of sole, which have been folded in half Right: adding hollandaise sauce to the dish after coating with white sauce

Country-style pâté 1 (pâté de campagne)

1 lb veal, or pork (minced)
8 oz pigs liver (minced)
4 oz pork fat (minced)
1 shallot (finely chopped)
1 large wineglass port wine
about $\frac{1}{4}$ of a small white loaf
 (crusts removed)
3 eggs (beaten)
small pinch of allspice (Jamaican
 pepper)
1 teaspoon marjoram, or thyme
 (chopped)
pinch of salt
6–8 rashers of streaky bacon
clarified butter (see Glossary)

Medium-size loaf tin

Method

Put the veal and pigs liver, pork fat and shallot into a bowl. Pour the port over the bread and leave until thoroughly soaked; add this to the meats with the beaten eggs, allspice, herbs and salt. Work together in electric blender, or beat thoroughly. Line the loaf tin with the bacon rashers, fill with the mixture and press well down. Smooth the top, cover with foil or tie on a double sheet of greaseproof paper. Cook in a bain marie for $1\frac{1}{4}$–$1\frac{1}{2}$ hours at 350°F or Mark 4. The pâté is cooked when firm to the touch. Press the pâté in the tin with a light weight (about 2 lb) and leave until cold. Then turn out and cut into slices for serving. To store, cover with a little clarified butter and keep in a cool place.

Country-style pâté 2 (pâté de campagne)

1 lb veal (minced)
8 oz raw ham (minced)
1 lb pork (minced)
8 oz pigs liver (minced)
6 oz pork fat (minced)
2 cloves of garlic (crushed)
good pinch of allspice (Jamaican
  pepper)
salt and pepper
1 wineglass brandy, or sherry
about 4 oz fat unsmoked bacon
1 bayleaf
clarified butter (see Glossary), or
  melted lard
luting paste (see page 47)

Terrine or oven-proof casserole

Method
Put minced meats and pork fat into a bowl, add the crushed cloves of garlic, allspice and seasoning. Moisten with the brandy or sherry.

Lay the fat bacon in the bottom of a terrine and put in the mixture. Press meat well down, smooth over the top and place the bayleaf on top. Put on the lid, seal with a luting paste and cook in a bain marie in the oven for about $1\frac{1}{2}$–$1\frac{3}{4}$ hours at 350°F or Mark 4 until pâté is firm to the touch.

Take out of oven, remove lid, press pâté under a moderate weight (about 2 lb). Leave until cold, then cover with clarified butter or melted lard, and keep in a cool place until wanted.

Pâté bretonne

3 herrings (filleted and
  skinned)
1–2 tablespoons lemon juice
1 tablespoon finely chopped
  herbs
$\frac{1}{4}$ teaspoon ground nutmeg
$\frac{1}{4}$ teaspoon ground allspice
salt and pepper
clarified butter (for serving)
  – see Glossary

For farce

2 herrings (filleted and
  skinned)
3 hard-boiled eggs
4 oz rice (cooked till tender
  in veal, or chicken, stock)
1 large mushroom (chopped)
1 egg (beaten)

Terrine or oven-proof casserole

Method
Set oven at 350°F or Mark 4.

Marinate the 3 filleted herrings in the
lemon juice, herbs, spices and seasoning
while preparing the farce.

Pound the 2 herrings with the yolks of
the hard-boiled eggs, mix in the cooked
rice and chopped mushroom and pass this
mixture through a fine sieve or Mouli.
Season and bind with the beaten egg.
Place half the mixture in a buttered terrine
and arrange the marinated fillets on top,
then cover with the remaining farce. Stand
the dish in a bain marie and cook in pre-set
oven for 45–50 minutes.

Leave to get cold and pour over a little
clarified butter before serving. Hand hot
toast and butter separately.

A terrine is a glazed earthenware casserole, traditionally used for cooking the
more substantial type of pâté.

Liver pâté

1½ lb pigs, or calves, liver
8 oz very fat bacon (unsmoked),
    or fat from cooked ham
2–3 tablespoons double cream
    (optional)
1 dessertspoon anchovy essence

For béchamel sauce

½ pint milk (infused with slice of
    onion, 6 peppercorns, 1 bayleaf,
    1 blade of mace)
1 oz butter
1 rounded tablespoon flour
salt
pepper (ground from mill)
pinch of ground mace, or nutmeg

*1 lb cake tin, or 6-inch diameter top
(No. 2 size) soufflé dish*

Pigs liver is excellent for pâtés,
being rich and well flavoured.
Calves liver is more expensive
but more delicate in flavour.

Method

Remove any ducts and cut liver
into small pieces. Take two-
thirds of the bacon or ham fat,
cut into small pieces and pass
all through a mincer and/or
work in an electric blender.

To make the béchamel
sauce: put milk and flavourings
to infuse. Melt butter in a pan,
stir in flour and gradually blend
in strained milk. Stir over heat
until boiling, then boil for 2
minutes. Season to taste, add
ground mace or nutmeg. Turn
into a dish and leave to cool.

Mix the liver with béchamel
sauce, cream and anchovy
essence. Slice the rest of the
bacon or ham fat and use to
line the bottom of the shallow
tin or soufflé dish.

If liver mixture is not very
smooth, pass it through a sieve

or mix in electric blender. Turn into tin or dish, cover with foil, set in a bain marie half-full of hot water. Bring to boil, then put in oven for 45–50 minutes at 350°F or Mark 4, until firm to the touch. Cover with grease-proof paper, a plate or board and put a light weight (about 2 lb) on top and leave until the next day. Turn out and cut in slices for serving. If pâté is to be kept for several days, cover top with a little clarified butter (see Glossary) and keep in a cool place.

Liver pâté is a good first course, served with hot buttered toast

Terrine maison

8 oz thin streaky bacon rashers
   (unsmoked)
8 oz shredded raw game (hare,
   rabbit, or pigeon, or lean pork,
   or raw gammon rasher)
1 small wineglass sherry, or port
   (optional)
1 bayleaf
$\frac{1}{4}$ pint jellied stock
luting paste (see page 47)

For farce

8 oz pigs liver (minced)
8 oz veal (minced)
8 oz fat pork (minced)
1 small onion (finely chopped)
1 dessertspoon fresh herbs
   (chopped), or $\frac{1}{2}$ this quantity if
   using dried herbs
salt and pepper

Method

Remove rind from bacon rashers and line them into a terrine. Work the minced meats and pork fat with the onion and herbs for farce. Season.

Pour the wine over the shredded game and season to taste. Layer about a third of the liver farce into the terrine. Press down well. Scatter half the shredded game on top and repeat these layers, ending with farce. Smooth the top and press on a bayleaf. Cover with lid and seal with luting paste.

Cook in a bain marie in the oven at 325°F–350°F or Mark 3–4 for $1\frac{1}{2}$–2 hours, or until firm to the touch. Remove lid, press well with a 4 lb weight. When cold, remove any fat round the sides and fill up with the jellied stock. Leave until set.

Above left: lining the terrine with bacon

Above centre: shredding the raw game

Above right: sealing the lid of the terrine with luting paste

Right: the terrine, ready to turn out and serve (see cover picture)

Terrine of pork

1 lb pork fillets
8 oz streaky bacon rashers
   (unsmoked)

For farce

1 small onion (finely chopped)
1 oz butter, or bacon fat
4 oz flat mushrooms (chopped)
1 dessertspoon fresh mixed herbs
   (chopped), or ½ quantity if dried
4 oz calves, or lambs, liver (minced)
4 oz pork (minced), or sausage
   meat
1 teacup of fresh white
   breadcrumbs
1 tablespoon brandy, or 2 of sherry
about 12 pistachio nuts (blanched
   and halved) – optional
salt
pepper (ground from mill)
luting paste (see opposite)

*Rectangular terrine, or medium-size
   loaf tin*

Method

Slit pork fillets and then beat
to flatten them out (the butcher
will do this for you). Remove
rind from bacon, spread out on
a board with a palette knife
and use to line base and sides
of a terrine or loaf tin.

To prepare farce: soften
onion in butter or bacon fat
and add chopped mushrooms.
Cook briskly for 3–4 minutes,
then add herbs and turn mixture on to a plate to cool. Add
minced liver to the minced pork
or sausage meat, the mushroom
mixture and breadcrumbs. Add
brandy or sherry and the pistachio nuts. Season well.

Put a third of the farce in
bottom of lined terrine or tin,
cover with half the pork fillets,
then add another layer of farce
and the rest of the fillets.

Cover with the remaining farce. If any bacon rashers are left, lay these on top of the farce. Put on the lid and seal with a luting paste of flour and water. If using a tin, cover with a double sheet of greaseproof paper and a sheet of foil.

Set in a bain marie and cook in the oven at 325°F or Mark 3 for $1-1\frac{1}{2}$ hours. Then press lightly (not more than 3–4 lb weight) until cold.

To serve, turn out and cut into slices about $\frac{1}{4}$-inch thick. Serve with salad.

To blanch pistachio nuts pour boiling water over the shelled nuts and add a small pinch of bi-carbonate of soda (this helps to preserve the colour). Cover the pan and leave until cool. Drain and rinse in cold water. The skins can then be removed easily.

Luting paste is a flour and water mixture of a consistency similar to that of scone dough. To seal a casserole or terrine, put 3–4 oz flour into a bowl and mix quickly with cold water to a firm dough (4 oz flour will take $\frac{1}{8}$ pint water).

Terrine of hare

1 hare
4 oz fat bacon, preferably larding
  bacon (in the piece)
1 wineglass port, or sherry
good pinch of ground allspice
  (Jamaican pepper), or mace
pepper (ground from mill)
2 shallots (finely chopped)
8 oz pork (minced)
8 oz sausage meat
1 dessertspoon mixed herbs
  (chopped)
salt and pepper
6 oz tongue (in 2 slices)
1 bayleaf
luting paste (see page 47)
strong jellied stock (made from
  hare bones with 1–2 veal bones,
  or a pig's trotter for good jell)

Method
Lift the fillets from the back of the hare with a sharp knife and cut into strips. Cut bacon into strips. Lay both in a dish, pour over the port or sherry, add spice, pepper and shallots. Cover, leave overnight.

Cut off all the meat from the rest of the hare, mince with its liver and add to the pork and sausage meat. Add herbs, season well and add any liquid from hare. Cut the tongue into strips and add to the hare fillets.

Press a third of the farce into a terrine and spread half of the marinated meat and tongue on top. Cover with half of remaining farce, then rest of the meat and finally, the remaining farce. Smooth top, press a bayleaf in centre, cover, seal lid with luting paste.

Cook in a bain marie in the oven at 325°F or Mark 3 for 2 hours. Remove lid, press overnight with a 4 lb weight, then fill up dish with stock.

University of Plymouth
Charles Seale Hayne Library
Subject to status this item may be renewed
via your Voyager account

http://voyager.plymouth.ac.uk
Tel: (01752) 232323